Follow Your Heart,

For It Always Leads You Home

Guidance Writings by

RoseAngel

www.roseangelguidance.com

ISBN 978-1-4675-6390-1

This book is dedicated to
Kim Blackberg who shared in my beliefs,
Karen Walsh who helped me every step of the way,
Christina Paffumi who believed in me,
Amanda Reaves who stood by my side and
Matt Reaves who has been my greatest supporter.

Introduction

I always had this drive to know why I was here. My life was not good and it was getting worse, and I knew in my gut this wasn't right. The worse it became, the more I wanted to understand. I knew I was a good person, relatively intelligent, clever even. I was strong in the manner that I didn't scare easily and even if I did, you would never tell by my face or actions. I tolerated a lot of deep level abuse in my life but that was all I ever knew so it was just survival to me. But through all of this, I knew I was missing something. I knew this wasn't what life was supposed to be about. So I searched for answers.

At first I thought I was searching for the meaning of life. I wanted to know why we were here and why did some have it good and others have it so bad. What was the purpose of so much suffering, even if there were the good times in between? I was lost, searching for the truth and nothing made sense. I didn't understand how I could work so hard and never make it any closer to having a happier life. I was missing something. Why did bad things keep following me? WHY IS THIS ALL SO HARD?

The meaning of life, I was told was 'Love'. Makes sense, I thought. Love can heal, love makes you happy, love makes you do things you don't even know why you are doing. Love is the answer I was searching for. There, I did it, I figured out the meaning of life. Whew, that's better. But, how do I love my way into a better life? And how do I get this 'Love' to work for me? I found myself back at step one.

Maybe it wasn't the 'meaning of life' I was searching for. Maybe I needed to know the purpose of life. There has to be a reason for our existence. We couldn't be existing without any meaning, could we? If there is no purpose, no goal; nothing to achieve or move toward... well, there has to be meaning to exist.

I started searching for answers in self-help books and they all seemed to agree that we were here for the experience and to learn. Learn what? What is it that I need to learn to make my life better and what lesson can I learn to take this pain away? I wondered if there was someone who could teach me to be happy with my life. Just tell me the answers and I will do it, anything to make it to the goal of a happy, prosperous life surrounded by a picket fence. But no matter how many books I read, seminars I went to or therapy sessions I attended, I couldn't figure out what I was doing wrong or what lesson that could be learned.

I was filled with unanswered questions, lost and searching for reasons why things were not turning out the way my life was supposed to be. I wanted to know who was responsible for dishing out all this bad luck. I am doing everything I am supposed to do, yet I keep finding myself in a ditch I have to climb my way out of just to be blindsided by the next one. I work so hard, I give up so much, I care for the ones I love... why isn't this life working for me?

My deep desires for answers lead me to learn to meditate. I was then able to tap into this inner voice that had been there all along. Now I had a way to get answers to all these unanswered questions I had bottled up inside of me. I didn't know where the voice was coming from or why, but I knew it eased my pain and many times helped me through my depression. What I didn't know at the time, is that you can have all the answers yet not be ready to intergrate the solutions.

'Follow Your Heart, For It Always Leads You Home' is a collection of answers I have been given from my many years of questions. I have learned so much from these years of guidance, mainly to keep a positive attitude because what you are thinking is a very powerful tool in creating your future. Concentrate on staying positive and focus on your desires being achieved, because you are always in the process of attracting your upcoming life experiences.

Chapter One

'Appreciation'

Some say appreciate the little things in life, we say appreciate big for it is creating your future.

You Choose, Appreciation Or Fear

Appreciation is very powerful you know, for it creates a path for your future events. If you appreciate something, then you are feeling the greatness of it. This is your focus and with focus comes realization of more of the same. This being said, what do you appreciate?

This is a difficult question for some. It is because their focus is on the lack and how are they going to continue without it. Please understand that what you concentrate on, especially with passion is what is relevant in your life. Do you want to feel what makes you happy or what you fear? This is your choice, you know. If we were you, we would choose happiness every time.

Now there are some who think this is just avoiding the truth. But are your future events really your truths? You create your future, if you are worrying it is always about the future... create a happy future. Appreciate what is good in life, do not give power in what is feared, and you will see that life becomes what you desired, and the fears you once had will have no power to exist.

I Would Like To Talk About Appreciation...

I would like to talk about appreciation. Wow, what a feeling it is to sit in pure appreciation of life. To see what we take for granted and to thank the Universe for having it. Then there is seeing the other side of what we feel we are lacking. To see the situation as healed and appreciating that. We all have the ability to change what we think is "wrong" in life. **We just can not dwell on the "wrong" and start to believe it can be "right" again.** Then there are the really bad situations that we go through in life. Experience shows that the worse it is, the greater the life change becomes, and the value of the overall experience is always worthy in the long run.

Appreciate The Little Things

Appreciation is so powerful it can literally change your life. When you see what is good in your life, this directs you to more of the same. When you see what is wrong in your life - well, it is depressing isn't it? Which would you rather choose? Some would say that this is just denying the facts, but we say this is choosing the outcome.

It makes sense when you think about it, what you believe in, is where your focus is upon. If you believe something, you are looking for it to happen and you will notice things that are similar. It is now in your attention and you will become aware of which path leads you toward this belief. If you believe that you will not receive something, maybe because your parents never had it, or you feel you are not good enough, or you think good things like that just don't happen to people like you, well then when something better becomes part of your experience, you will not move toward it for you feel you are not worthy.

So we ask you to appreciate the little things and do not give your attention to the problems. Little by little you will start to notice more good things and you will see that your life is not all bad. You will look forward to what good you do have and before you know it, you will attract more and more happy experiences to you. For you will understand how to accept more good in your life and you will no longer feel that bad things happen by chance.

Appreciation... Why Does It Work?

Appreciation - What is it all about? How does it work? Why would it work? Seriously, how can it be that simple? These questions are often associated with the thoughts of appreciation making a difference in people's lives. We are here to explain why. We are attraction people, meaning what we do, think and believe attracts more of that to our experiences. It's all about energy. Scientifically it has been proven that everything is energy so why is this so hard to believe? Energy moves toward more energy like itself. So, put it all together and it is clear, wherever we focus our energy will attracts more of the same.

If you focus on appreciation, then what you appreciate in life will multiply, it is law. If you focus on the lack in your life, by the same law, your lack will multiply. This being said... What do you want to put your energy toward?

Chapter Two

'Belief'

Thoughts equal belief, belief equals ability, ability equals confidence, confidence diminishes doubt.

The Sky Is The Limit

The sky is the limit... what do you think this means? And why are you accepting limits, dear one? The sky is a great start but how did we learn to go out into space if we limit ourselves to the sky?

We want you to follow your heart, no matter how far it guides you to move toward a dream. Your belief in limits is the only thing keeping you from achieving your dreams, you know.

So many times we stop ourselves from believing we can achieve our dreams and we want you to know that this is not your true belief. You have been told or you may have witnessed someone else who was not able to achieve their desires and you then chose to believe it was not possible.

We say if you believe and would work toward this belief, it has to manifest, for your true beliefs are everything. They shape your life, accomplish your goals and create your reality.

Does This Feel Good?

Hello dear ones, how do you feel? Do you know how important the answer to this question is? How you feel is an indication of what your life is creating, you know. Many of you do not understand or believe this, we know, but it is true. You see, what you believe in life is what you focus on, and what you focus on is what you are drawn to, and what you are drawn to is what you see to be the truth. How can you create something you do not believe to be true?

The problem most have is that they have been drawn to believe that they can not have, or they do not deserve, or even that so many desires are just out of their reach. And we say, no! There is nothing you can not have or do, you know. The life inside of you is capable of creating anything the person desires.

Think about what you want, feel it to be true, do not doubt for a moment (for you will lose your connection to it) and then just understand it is on its way. No worries for you know it is happening.

Once you can do this, then your belief will become your point of attention and it will be.

Desire Is Not What Most Think It Is

Desire can never be a bad thing, even if it is something that may hurt another. Most have not learned that nothing bad can happen to them unless it is allowed by them. This being said, bad things that happen to good people are the desires of those good people unto themselves. This is difficult for most to grasp for we

19

have been taught that if we are good, good things are given to us. Has this belief ever really come true to any good person?

Quit judging yourselves, believe you deserve good things happening to you and accept others as they are, for you are not them and it is not your job to fix them.

What Do You Believe?

Simply said, if we do not believe, we stop the thought of achieving, for in our mind it is not possible. How can you see yourself with something that is not possible? The mind, body, thought, belief and energy of creation are all connected. They are all the same, they all work together.

Define God Please –

God is what you make of Him/Her. For some do not believe in God, and if there is no belief, there is not benefit of belief. We are all God and we all have choices to tap into our God given powers, but if we do not believe, there is no direction to create with the gifts we have.

If you believe in God, then God is only as strong as your belief. If you believe in miracles, then miracles can happen. If you believe in healing, then healing can happen. If you believe you are taken care of, then you are. So God is what you believe God is (for we have all agreed on free choice). All this being said, God is all there is and nothing at all, it is all up to you.

What Do You Believe In?

What do you believe in? That is where you start. We all believe in something that is a step above where we are now. We can believe in "The rich become richer". So how does that help someone who does not believe they will ever be rich? You break it down until it matches your belief of yourself. It can start like this... What are you thinking when you see "the rich" buying something? Listen to your thoughts, are you putting them down – Rich people are not happy people, Rich people think they are better than everyone else, Rich people can not buy love, etc. Now, you have somewhere to start. **If you believe the rich are not good or happy people, then you are telling yourself that in order to stay good or happy, you have to live in lack of money.** This is not true! There are many good and happy rich people. There are many bad and unhappy poor people. Your emotions and choice of being has nothing to do with money.

What Is Alignment And How Do We Get There?

Alignment is the complete acceptance o f who you are, what you are, and what you want, with the complete acceptance that it is yours. When you are aligned, everything comes to you easily. This is how it is supposed to be. We are not supposed to struggle or fight for what is justly ours. We have been trained to work hard, but this does not have to be, we choose it to justify receiving. Once we understand that receiving is our birthright, then everything will fall into place. You are complete energy, every one of you deserve what you accept into your alignment. In other words, you deserve what you believe you deserve. Believe big and receive big, believe bad and receive bad, etc. Your Higher Energy wants you to believe you deserve peace, joy and happiness but so many believe they are not deserving of this, and their lives follow their beliefs. We as a planet need to think differently, believe we deserve good and feel comfortable accepting the good in our lives.

The Power Of Belief

What we believe, we achieve. Why? Because we are focusing on a solution or a creation. We are putting our power into what is possible or what is believed. Let's face it, if we do not believe, we do not try. The effort is eliminated because we believe it is not possible. But if we believe, well then we know there is a chance or more, maybe a reality of possibility. Now see this, we try to accomplish or create or bring into our lives what is believed. Our thoughts are working toward this goal, our belief is that it can be done and our energy is attracting it into our existence. This is not possible if we do not believe. Nonbelief is the end of the possibility of creating.

Chapter Three

'Choice'

You can not change the way others
act toward you, you can only change
how you react to it.

We See Things The Way We Want

Here we go again; we are either happy or sad, and have not figured out that being in between is a better state, for then we are not creating that which is not wanted, you know.

When we are sad, we will find things to support our feelings, for being sad is a choice and seeing the good all around us does not confirm that chosen state of mind. This is why so many now use the term 'think positive'. For when you look for the positive in any given situation, it opens a door of choice, and usually a better choice than what you are living at the time.

Being happy is also a choice. It usually takes more energy to do so since others do not want to see you in your contentment when they are choosing to be sad.

All we are asking is to be aware of your state of mind and if it does not bring you joy, happiness or even contentment, then choose to change it. Just focus on one little thing that makes you happy, feel it and then you will feel it dissolve your sadness enough to be open to other happy feelings.

Which Is The Path To Least Resistance?

Everything we do, everything we decide, every step we walk is the choice of our path to least resistance. What do we mean by this? We find ourselves in situations we do not like, such as a bad job, a painful relationship, or overwhelmed by family or friends. We pray for change but the change we ask for is not the choice we wanted for you have already chosen to be in this situation.

We think we are trapped in a bad job but we chose it. Hard to believe, we know, but think about it; if the negative outweighed the positive, you would be out of there. You stay because of the money or because there are not any good jobs out there or our personal favorite, because you like the people you work with. This job is the path to least resistance and that is why you are still working there. Once you focus on the good aspects of the job and let go of the bad, then you will become happy at work once again. Either at this job, or another job that will open up to you.

The same with your relationships, you continue to 'suffer' through them because the good outweigh the bad. Whatever the reasons (and there are so many), once the bad outweighs the good, which you usually call 'rock bottom', then change will be made.

So it all comes down to what you are focusing on, dear one for you are exactly where you want to be in life, otherwise you would have changed it.

The Circle Of Life

Dear ones, we have been guiding you to pay attention to your thoughts and feelings for this is the direction your life will move toward. Most of you understand this and some of you do not, but you still work on thinking positive and we say this works well, for being positive creates more positive moments in life.

Now the confusion sets in when you know how you want to think and believe, and you find yourself in life situations that seem to all move toward pain and frustration. It is easy to forget that by being sad or angry, that you are creating more of the same. When this happens it tends to become more overwhelming, for your beliefs are supporting more of the same. And you do not understand why so many upsetting things tend to all happen at once, and we say dear one, this is your choice. By choosing to be upset, angry or sad (even though the life situation mirrors these emotions), you are creating more of the same. The universe works to give you what you believe, so if you are not happy with what you are creating, we say change it.

28

We know this does take much effort on your part, for you are not in the mood to 'be happy' when life is dishing out such sad events but again, remember it is all about choice. We ask you to stop, breathe deeply and release your breath slowly... accept the calmness and remember what is good in life. There is always good in life no matter how sad things are, but it is up to you to focus on them. It could be as simple as a sunny day, a hot shower, a roof over your head or your favorite pair of shoes. Simple, we know but there are things that may make you happy.

Understand dear ones, you always have a choice, and what you choose to focus on is everything.

Why Allow Another To Change Who You Are?

Hello dearest one - why worry about that which does not serve you? Why allow others to decide your feelings and most of all dear one, why allow another to change who you are?

You are blinded by your feelings, and we say *it is so much easier to be yourself.* No worries of what is said about you for you know who you are. No worries that others will believe that which is not true, for you do not need to defend yourself when you truly believe in yourself.

Take a deep breath and remember who you are. Send love to the ones who bring you pain, for by doing this you release yourself of the control they have on you. Do not live in reaction to others, for they are misguiding you. Be yourself in the midst of chaos, and allow yourself to feel the calm. Today, dear one, you are in charge of your own feelings and this will set you free.

Life Is Funny

Life is funny sometimes, not the haha funny but the hmmm, I did not see that coming funny. People think they want things in life easy and well-adjusted but this is not true. If it were true, why would so many create such dramatic lives? This is not by accident that people fall into this type of life. This is chosen, maybe not consciously, but we always have choices. Life may seem tiring at times, you may just want to give up but at these times, dear ones, your energy to heal is at its highest, and this is a good thing. Everything is balanced and what seems to be difficult is just the opportunity to make different choices or to learn by trial and error.

We are always growing, learning and expanding our minds and souls and there is not one of us that would have it any other way. It all comes down to how you experience your difficult times, that is the key, you know. Choose to try something different, choose to not allow it to sadden or affect other aspects of your day, choose to see the other side of the situation. For when you can accomplish this, life's burdens will cease to have an effect on your life.

Take A Deep Breath Of Freedom

Freedom is like fresh air, there is no question what to do and how it feels. Freedom is salvation. When you are truly free, everything works out for you. This is because you have nothing to hide behind so you have to be honest with yourself. If you are honest with yourself and something is not working out, you would not blame yourself for this is not who you are, you would try something else until it did work for you. There is no room for blame when you are free. Blame is the cowardly way to say you messed up so that you can end something you are not happy with. If there was no blame and what happened just happened, then you would take the next step to change it, if it is something you do not like.

Addiction Is A Choice

Addiction is a choice, yes this is true. Because one chooses it to discover a way to cope with things that are difficult to face. This is why it is more comfortable than wanting to change.

Addictions are not bad things, as you believe. They sometimes save you from losing control of your mind.

Escape is sometimes like a well needed vacation. Once the vacation ends, you are rested enough to face reality again, but with a new perspective.

You've heard of hitting rock bottom. Well, rock bottom is the point where it is more comfortable to face the fear than to escape into an addiction that brings you pain. It is all good, for sometimes this is what is needed to see the other side is not so bad.

Tell Me My Future

Your future is forever changing, depending on where you are in life. We are not here to tell you something that is not written in stone, but we are here to guide you to the happiness you deserve.

Follow your gut for it leads you to what is desired in life. **Do not dwell on mistakes** for they teach you what is not wanted, and expands the desire not to feel that way again. **Believe in yourself** for anything is possible, if you believe it is. **Trust that life is what you make of it** and you will in turn make it fun.

Chapter Four

'Direction'

Quit judging yourselves, believe you deserve good things happening to you and accept others as they are, for you are not them and it is not your job to fix them.

Why Worry?

We find ourselves in a fearful situation and our first reaction is to worry, and we ask why worry about the unknown? And why worry about that which you can not change? The reason we worry is because life has taken us to directions which we are not comfortable in, and we think it is just going to become worse. This is where we disagree, you know for you can choose to change it.

Why believe something you do not know is going to become worse? Why believe anything other than figuring out how to feel better? There are choices in everything you do, why choose failure?

What we focus on is the direction we will head, it is inevitable you know. What you think about is what is to come, for we see nothing else. We say focus on the possibilities that please you, not that which worries you. For you will find a way to change your circumstance, whether it be for the worse or for the better. It is always your choice.

Who am I?

You are who you want to be. You are who you believe you are. This being said, who do you want to be? It is that easy, you know. There are so many things that stop you

34

from achieving your dream, but in reality there is only one thing that stops you and it is you.

Listen to what calls you. How does this make you feel? This will determine if you are ready. Sometimes we want to be ready but are paralyzed in fear. Why, you think, could something as natural as following your calling be so scary?

Scary is just your separation from your real self, you know. Scary is what you use for the reason to not move forward. Fear not, for you have nothing to lose unless you do not try. Dreams are here for the taking and worthiness has nothing to do with it.

It is us who call you toward your dreams, for it is you who desires change. Move forward dear ones, for we will be with you every step of the way.

Life's Direction

Dearest one, what direction are you heading to? Are you happy with that which you are creating? Do you feel joy and enthusiasm regarding your future, or do you feel trapped?

You create your life, believe it or not. Your thoughts are outlining your direction and if you feel no hope, then your life will follow.

You say, this is how it is and we say that is how it was. You say you have no luck and we say you create your own luck. You say why would something good ever happen to me and we say why not?

It all starts with a thought – think better. What little possibility could you see for yourself? What small change are you willing to take? What negative belief are you not going to allow to surface?

When you are ready to change your direction, start small and enjoy the changes for when you feel joy, the possibility of moving in the right direction opens up for you.

Dreams Create Your Future

Why worry? You know this does not serve you. Why not dream big for your dreams are creating your future. Why think things are hard to achieve when you know this ends any quest you may want. Life is not as hard as you make it out to be, you know.

You are so busy reacting to life, that you forget you are creating your future. Take a deep breath and enjoy what you have. What pleases you brings more of the same into your living days.

Spend more time doing what you enjoy, spend less time worrying about what you do not have. This is the key to happiness, you know.

What is Freedom?

Freedom is being yourself. When you are free you are growing, learning, succeeding, and being the only person you really know. Don't you want to know yourself? Some do not, but that is just because they do not like themselves. The truth is, we would all like ourselves if we understood ourselves. This leads us back to freedom to be ourselves.

Life is a Journey

Trust that all roads lead to your desired destination and do not hesitate to take a wrong turn once in a while for it is those detours that bring you the most experiences in validation of what is truly wanted. And it is also those experiences that get you back on the path of true desire. So many want to be right, or want to accomplish their goals the quickest. And in doing so would give up the true value of being on this journey in the first place.

Chapter Five

'Fear'

Worrying sends doubt, doubt creates fear, fear takes over thoughts, and once you think it can not be done, it won't.

Do What Makes You Scared

So dear one, you are confronted with something that scares you and then you stop. We say this is not an indication of fear, it is an indication of not having the confidence to try. There is a big difference, you know.

When you think the situation out and find reasons not to move forward, we ask you to listen to these reasons. Are they fear based because of the unknown? Are they excuses that can be considered opinionated? Are there sad endings to the story you make up in your mind?

This is normal, we know for you have lost your guidance and replaced it with the voices of your past. You were born confident and all-knowing of your power. Along the way, others have told you that your actions were bad or dangerous, or not the way society likes you to act. This creates fear in place of the confidence you once understood.

So we ask you dear one to do what makes you scared, for your power still lives inside of you and you deserve to know your true strength.

Feeling Stuck

We all have desires, yet most of us are afraid to confront them. It is not that we fear the outcome, it is we fear change or going against what we've been taught or what others would approve of. This puts us in the middle, or feeling 'stuck'. There is nothing that bothers oneself more than feeling stuck, for we know what we want and we can not get there.

There are reasons for these feelings, most too complicated to explain. We are all in the process of experiencing life, and in order to do so, there are many levels that must be accomplished in order to move toward what is wanted. The reason for the levels is because you can not go from one belief to another without experiencing the shift or change, and then the belief that it is possible.

For example, you want to learn to dance but all your life you believe you have two left feet. You can not go from that belief to the belief that you are a great dancer. You start out small and once you accomplish a simple step, you are confident to try the next and so on, until you become what you believe you can be.

This is true for everything in life, it is just that most want it all, and they want it now. Let go dear ones and appreciate what you do have, and then just take the next step.

Fear Is One Of The Greatest Sins Against Thy Self

Fear is a very binding emotion, it truly is one of the greatest sins against the self. There can never be any good that comes from a fearful situation but it goes so much further than that.

Fear is the opposite of love, hands down. It starts inside of the self and in order to try and control it, it is used outside the self. In other words, it may start as an uncomfortable thought. This thought brings you into a direction where more like thoughts begin to surface. As the fear grows, it binds you. You see no way out, so you learn to deal with it, or so called, control it. Though fear can never be controlled, it can be released (in the beginning it will keep returning, just to be released again). It is hard to release fear on your own, yet it is even harder to share your fear with someone for help, because you have to feel the loss of control.

Judge Not

Some think those who are not in a good place in life are weak and lazy, though to live a life of undesirable existence, you have to be strong in order to ignore the signs for change. We are not saying that this is a desired experience; we are just saying that it is strength and maybe stubbornness to live that which is not wanted, and not try to change. We probably have you very confused right now because this is the opposite of what you have been taught all your life. That is because their strength is powered by their fear of changing, and fear is looked down upon.

Fear is an amazing emotion, when learned early in life, one will find mechanisms to fight against it. Those in life that are not living their dreams because they are so strong are usually the ones who learned their strengths from surviving fearful experiences at a young age. They ,have lived through life having others more fortunate look down upon them to the point that they also believe in their failure. This is a lesson that is the most difficult to overcome, for it is an ongoing cycle in life that has created an acceptance within. Once they can break through this fear and step out of their comfort zone of acceptance, these are the people who will accomplish the most in life.

Facing Your Fear

The only way to release fear is to face it for what it really is; which is usually a misinterpretation of a situation in life that we were not able to understand when we originally lived through it. In other words, a big misunderstanding. Say, as a child, you witnessed someone get hurt, either on their own or by the hand of another. You are fearful that you may fall victim to the same scenario. When anything happens in your present day that reminds you of this past situation, you relive the fear of the child that experienced that situation. You do this because as a child you did not understand, and as an adult you do not go past the fear feeling to see this misinterpretation. That is what is meant by facing your fear. Once you get past the overwhelming feeling of fear, and the truth behind the fear materializes, there is nothing left to be afraid of. **You understand it and it no longer has power over you.**

The Power Behind Fear And Guilt

Fear and guilt are the only two true sins, for you can only sin upon yourself. When you believe you are a victim and that bad things happen to you, well then you are creating your future thoughts and actions. These actions multiply for you feel you have no choice to change. We want you all to know, there is always a choice, always. If not, then why do people who hit "rock bottom" turn their lives around and become the person they have always desired to be?

Guilt works about the same, as it binds you in belief that you are wrong for wanting good in your life. This also will snowball into deeper guilt, for your inner self knows you deserve better. So when you choose guilt to stop from helping yourself to live a better life, well the signs become stronger and more difficult to live through. Until you are not able to live with it and then fight back. Or in some cases, give up. Guilt and fear are always emotions which will hold you back from moving forward in life, always. Only you can make your life better or happier, and only you can stop the flow of good into your life. Life is full of choices, which choices are you making?

Where Do I Find Freedom?

Freedom is the release of fear and guilt. That just feels good to say... Freedom is the Release of Fear and Guilt. Fear and guilt are terrible, painful, harmful, ongoing sins against the self. If everyone were able to release all fear and guilt there would truly be a world without prisons, wars or prejudice. Think about this, all sins against ourselves or others are fear based – All Sins! If there is no fear, there is no reason to harm yourself or others. People steal because of fear of lack of money. People fight because of fear of being hurt themselves. Fighting is a control issue and if you feel out of control it is because you are afraid of the situation that is happening that you are trying to control. The truth is, you can only control your own actions. You may think you can fear someone into doing what you want, but sooner or later they will become stronger and take back their birthright to choose their own direction.

Losing A Loved One Is Very Difficult

Losing a loved one is very difficult for many. There is emptiness where life with this person used to exist. It seems unfair and sometimes scary. The pain can be so great that it is hard to go on with your normal life. We ask you to feel the pain, but not let the pain take over. Grief is an important part of life. We need it to balance our emotions, but some allow it to take over their feelings and then can easily become lost in the pain. When this happens, it is hard to reason and learn to live again.

Stop and think why you are so sad, for it is not for the loved one but for your pain. Your loved one wants you to be happy again, they want you to move on. It is you who chooses not to balance your loss with your life. We are not saying to be happy when we know you are not, we are asking you to feel the grief and then move on. There is so much and so many in everyone's life to be appreciative for. Bring yourself to focus on those things a little each day. Do something or talk to someone who brings a smile to your face, and little by little you will learn to live again. This also will allow your loved one to work with your from the other side.

Life has changed for you and it will continue to change for this creates growth, knowledge and experience. Life will never be the same, we know but life can be good again.

46

Chapter Six

'Growth'

We are all growing, learning and experiencing life, if we choose to or not. For without growth, there is no direction and we would have no reason to exist.

Oh What Little Faith We Actually Have

Hello dear ones, we are so pleased to talk to you today. We have been listening to your prayers and see your efforts to do what you have been told is the 'right thing' in order to assure your place in heaven, and we say stop trying so hard for we love you and we will always be here for you.

You have been trained to obey, and we never asked that of you. Obeying goes against all your beliefs, and then you are taught this is called faith. **This saddens us for faith is belief in thy self, not belief in other's opinions.** We are within you, always guiding you, yet you put a title on this inner guidance so that you may do what others tell you to do.

True faith dear ones, is the belief you have in yourself. True faith is the joy that you are always taken care of, even if you make the wrong choices. True faith is knowing you are always headed in the right direction even if you sway in order to experience life.

Life is so much easier than what we make of it. We want others to make the rules in order for us to feel we are doing the right thing. This does not serve you dear one, for what is right for one is not necessarily right for you. Go out and experience life, do what brings you joy and accept that this may not always have the best outcome.

Though if you choose to learn from these experiences, then you will grow stronger and more confident in yourself. This is what brings us joy, for in your growth we expand also, for in your joy, we feel your love, for in your misguidance, we too learn other choices.

Let go of your fears for life is an experience. There are not right or wrong choices, just life experiences. The more experiences you choose, the more you understand your purpose in life. And once you follow your purpose, your understanding of life will be so relevant that you will never question your chosen direction again.

So You Are Saying These Obstacles Are My Friends?

You want the money, you want the relationship, you want perfect health, you want success but you don't want to wait another moment for it all. You have been working on your life long enough to know how to create what is wanted, but yet you find yourself continuously running into obstacles from receiving it and we say No! No! No!

The obstacles you are receiving are what you are asking for, for they are your maps to achieving your dreams, you know. You want the money but what is it dear one that is keeping you from receiving it? Unless you change your alignment to be open to receive, it will always be there waiting for you, but just out of reach. The obstacles that you believe are in the way of receiving, actually hold the answer to receive. For you are creating these situations to show what you have to work through in order to accept what you are wanting. If you secretly think people with money are bad, then why would you really want the money that would make you bad? Same with the relationships, if you do not trust people, how would you be able to find someone in a loving relationship that you do not trust?

So next time you find yourself repeating life situations, or obstacles that are keeping you from your goals in life, work it through, for they are here to help you overcome what is not wanted, in order to allow what is wanted.

Why Am I Not Following My Dreams?

So you know what you want, yet you are not doing it, and we say why? What is it that holds you back from following your dreams?

We are all here to experience life, and we all agreed to follow our dreams. So if you are not following your dream, then you are in it only for the experience you receive. The problem with this, is since you are not moving in the right direction, the experience is usually not a peaceful one.

This is okay, for things that do not happen easily, make us aware of what is not wanted. When you know what is not wanted, you understand what is wanted. Once you reach your limit of what is not wanted, then you will move toward your goals.

This seems like the hard way to achieve something, we know but it is for the experience you receive along the way, which is more beneficial than the actual achievement of what is wanted.

Drama Queen

What is drama and why do we feel stuck in it at times? Drama is just confusion of life, not knowing where to turn to or why so many things are happening to you at once. This is a simple emotion, very helpful when life tends to come at you all at once. This confusion just means you are working through change, and change is important to your growth.

Drama is usually viewed as a negative situation but we say it is very positive. It represents change, and usually for the better. Though any change is good, for it points you in life to movement and direction. We are constantly changing, though we tend to want to stay in what we feel is comfortable. This does not work, for life will cause you to change. This is when the drama may occur, for you are fighting what your inner self is directing you to do.

Dear ones, do not view your drama or confusion of life negatively. For this is what is needed when you are ready to grow. So you have been called a drama queen and you wonder why is it that you sometimes feel this way?

We say as queen, you are the head leader of the land. It is a very important person that leads the people, you know. So put them together and you have a leader of confusion. We know this does not sound very impressive, but it is. Confusion means you are working through change, and change is important to your growth.

So the next time you are called a drama queen, thank them, for you know you are growing in life.

Chapter Seven

'Guidance'

When you blame others for what is going wrong in your life, you become a victim and lose your power to allow your own life changes.

You Ask, But Forget To Listen To The Answer

We always answer you but at times it seems you send out your request for guidance just to let it go, not understanding we want you to know the answer. Some call it prayers, others know it is guidance, for that is what we do. We never give you answers for you have free will to decide what to do, so we always guide you toward that which serves you.

When you are in pain, it seems easy to ask, hoping the answer will solve the problem. But we say there is no answer, only direction. You can choose to go in the direction of least resistance, or you may choose the direction that brings you more incentive for change. Either way, sooner or later you come to the point in life where it no longer serves you to be in pain, and you will pull yourself up to accept the change you feared.

Change is scary, for the unknown brings fear. Even when the known is completely painful, the unknown is equally full of fear. Guidance usually causes change, and you will do anything not to change that which is broken, for you have mastered working with the broken situation. The problem is that your inner guidance knows you deserve better than broken life experiences, so little by little it become relevant that change is needed.

We are all working together here, you know. We all want the same for each other, and that is to be in alignment with your wants and desires. This brings happiness, joy, peace, inner love and freedom. We are all on a journey to achieve these feelings, though many get lost on the way. Fear not for we are always here for you, whispering in your ear, sending you messages, reminding you of what you really desire in life, and that is the achievement of these desires, dear ones.

Why Do We Judge Others?

So we sit back and look at what we do not like in others, and we call this justification, for the norm does not act that way. We stay in our little world and act as others will approve of us to be, and we scold the ones who do not do the same. We do this sometimes in the name of God, and we say, do not pretend to know God in this way. Do not think that God judges His/Her children for you are not receiving this guidance from God.

Do you not want a God who is all loving? Do you believe that God offers you free will, and then judges you to experience this type of living? You believe God becomes angry when you do not obey Him/Her, yet you believe He/She is pleased with your control issues?

We are all individuals, we all came here to experience different lives. We are all children, learning, loving, becoming ourselves. We are all loving people, some who have lost their ways. We are here to find peace within ourselves and as long as we are pointing fingers at those who are different, we will never learn not to point fingers at ourselves. For in judging others, we judge ourselves.

In expecting others to follow the 'rules', we expect ourselves to do the same... and who made up these rules anyway? Certainly not the loving God that you follow.

Listen To Jack And Jill

There is a story of Jack and Jill. Jack brought Jill up a hill to fetch a pail of water, Jack fell down and broke his crown and Jill came tumbling after. Now, let's think of this... first of all, how many wells are on a hill? Next, if Jill did not have a pail, why did she follow Jack up the hill? Now, don't even get me started on the little boy who broke his crown. We know this as a fairy tail, that is believed to be suited for children but we ask, how does this story benefit the children?

We sometimes become so use to what we have been told, that we forget to question it. This also pertains to Gods and Religions, you know. We all have this amazing guidance within ourselves but forget how to use it. We would like

56

to know why there are so many who pray, if they are not willing to listen to the answers. They believe they are open to hearing, but if it is not within the limits of what they believe the answer to be, then they will not hear it.

We ask you all to be open to other possibilities of awareness, for life is not as complicated as many make it. Life is simple, but not always easy. Pay attention dear ones, listen, for your inner guidance will always set you in the direction to the happiness you are here to experience.

I Was Blind, But Now I See

We ask for guidance, pretending that we do not have infinite guidance within ourselves. We pray for answers, but we already know the answer we are avoiding. We cry for help, but deny ourselves relief, for we do not want to do what we know is that which we ask for.

Dear ones, life is an experience and sometimes we suffer unnecessarily, for we want to learn that which guides us to the peace that we so want to create. Why would we do this? Why would we choose pain over peace? Why do we want that which brings us suffering, when we can easily choose joy?

Some call it being lost, others call it depression or bad luck. Whatever you choose to call it, we want you to know it is all guidance. Take notice if you are experiencing pain, (we would categorize this as very strong guidance) for this only happens when you have ignored the subtle guiding.

So why would guidance hurt so? You choose to ignore the signs, and since you are always moving toward eternal growth, well... the signs become stronger and if necessary, more painful to get your attention, you know.

If you find yourself sad, lost or depressed, you are being guided to change your focus. For what you are thinking is bringing you pain, then it does not serve you. Pain is always either focus in the past, (which can not be changed) or focus in the future (which has not happened and may not ever happen). Live in the present, focus on the good in your life, see what pleases you, and do not give your attention to something that brings you pain or fear, for that leads you away from eternal growth.

Follow Your Inner Guidance

We all have inner guidance, enough to answer every question, enough to guide us to well being and enough to create the lives we dream of. We all have inner guidance but most do not follow it for they do not believe in it, or in themselves.

If you desire to be successful, though you believe that would never happen to someone like you, well then you will not follow your guidance, for you believe it must not be true.

We forget how powerful we all are. We forget that we were all born equal with the ability to create anything we desire. We become lost on the way and start to follow the beliefs of others. When you are so set on doing what others believe is good, or what others feel are the right things to do, then you lose touch with your own inner beliefs and your ability to create becomes distorted.

Be true to yourself, trust your emotions, follow your intuition and do not give your power to others beliefs for they do not know you, nor do they have any power over you unless you give it up to them.

Take A Good Look At Yourself

When you feel you are out of control, you really are making your control. When you fear the way the world looks at you, then you are looking at yourself with the most judgment of all. If you want to change, you will change. If you want to change so the world likes you, then you will always be resistant.

Your time to see yourself for yourself is now. The piece you are missing is the respect for yourself, just the way you are. The love for yourself, even though you are not perfect. The understanding that people are always doing the best they can, from what they have taken, from where they have come from – and this has never been a reflection on you. You alone know why you do the things you do, and where you are heading, regardless to what you look like.

Chapter Eight

'Happiness'

Trust that life is what you make of it,

and you will in turn make it fun.

How To Choose Happiness When You Are Feeling Sad

You ask this as if it is difficult, dear one and we say it never is. Happiness is your birthright and not choosing it is a decision and not the other way round. There is only happiness, though we choose to believe otherwise for various reasons.

We set such high goals and when they do not manifest, we choose to be sad. When in actuality we should not have given our strength to the thought that we were finished. Goals are ongoing, they are always accomplished, but they may not happen in the time frame planned. A goal is never failed, for it lives inside you and will resurface when it is time to work toward it again.

We sometimes choose to be 'sad' so that we can define why things are not turning out the way we want, whether it is a relationship, lack of money, feeling stuck in a situation or just not getting your way. When we choose to be sad, we are giving up on our dreams because that is easier than working toward the accomplishment of them.

Be open to what is wanted, do not ask for specifics for that will close you off to what is truly wanted. Look at the goal and not the lack of it. Feel what is wanted, but do not put a face on it. You are truly blessed at all times and being happy is easy when the meaning of sadness is understood. Remember we are always with you, guiding you, believing in you and once you see yourself the way we do... happiness becomes the choice.

What Makes You Tick

Hello dear ones, we are pleased to speak to you today about what we are all part of, and that is our inner tick. What makes you tick, we ask, knowing it is different in all of us. We all have something that guides us, be it intelligence, training, practice or even fear.

We all have direction from something we learned during our lives. We say, if you truly want to find joy in your life, forget what was learned and choose to listen to your inner guidance instead.

We all have the option to change the way things come into our lives. If you are not happy, it is probably because you are not feeling the freedom to be yourself. Happiness is a choice, and when we put others before ourselves we choose not to be free or most times not happy. We do this for selfless reasons, we know, but giving up for others is foolish, for we are the only ones who can create happiness in our lives. By giving up your freedom or happiness to assure other's happiness is senseless, it just can not be done.

So when your inner tick pulls you away from the joy in your life, remember you decide your direction and choices, the tick is just the recordings from the past and not necessarily what serves you.

How To Be Happy

Oh, such an amazing subject, so simple and so difficult at the same time. Happiness is the answer to the changes you are seeking. But to go from fear and worry to happiness can sometimes be a process. We are here to help you every step of the way, but you have to want it.

Who does not want to be happy? You think this is you but chances are, it is not. We want to be right more than we want to be happy. We want revenge for being wronged more than we want to be happy. We want our way, right or wrong more than we want to be happy. So this being said, what are you willing to give up to be happy? Seems silly, but in general most are not willing to give up the control of what is and the memory of what has wronged them to find the happiness they desire.

Choose to be happy, no matter what, just for one day, one week and then one month and your energy will line up with your desires. Your focus on what is good will have to surface and happy will no longer carry such resistance for then it must be.

Life is Supposed to Be Fun, You Know

Life is simple but some like to make it difficult. Life is fun but some look down on this. Life is exciting and adventurous but some do not find this to be safe. We ask you to look at how your life is working out for you. If you work at a job for a paycheck only, do you have enough to pay the bills? If you are in a relationship because you fear being alone, is there joy in your life? If you take care of others and put yourself last, do you feel satisfied in your living?

Many have living backwards, and we say stop, for this does not serve you. Many are so programmed to do what 'needs' to be done that they are blinded by it never really getting done. Slow down, take a deep breath and look at your life lovingly. Is fear stopping you from your true desires? Step out of your comfort zone and add fun in your life and then see how living is meant to feel like.

Chapter Nine

'Law of Attraction'

Like attracts like.

It begins with an idea, which in turn becomes a belief, and that which you believe without doubt must manifest, it is law.

But I Tried So Hard

If the Law of Attraction works when you believe in something, so why did I not get my belief? I tried so hard to believe it, yet it never came. And we say, if you are trying then you do not understand belief.

When you believe in something, then it is a done deal, no need to try or to hope or wait to see what happens because you *know* it is taken care of.

The Law of Attraction simply states, that which you believe, must be, for it is you who creates that which you are experiencing in this lifetime. This being said, you will see the emphasis is on 'belief' for it directs your experiences.

If you are not attracting that which is wanted, it is because your belief or your wanting is attached to something else in your experience, good or bad. Take your focus off that which does not please you and put it on that which brings you joy, dear one.

The Law of Attraction, Part I

The Law of Attraction is evident if you believe in it or not. It states that what you think about, feel within and believe to be true, will be attracted to your experiences in life. This is hard for some to understand for they believe that life is all by chance. Some are lucky, some are unlucky and things just happen to them without any control of how or where it comes from.

The good part is that you do have control over your life, in fact you attract everything into your experience. What do you believe about yourself? Where do you see yourself? What do you think of others? How are your finances, love life and health? Listen very careful how you answer, for these are your future experiences. If we were you, we would change our answers to be what is desired in life.

The Law of Attraction, Part II

When we realize that every thought we think, every word we speak and every emotion we experience is a request to the universe, then we can think, speak and eventually experience accordingly. For what is believed is always given to us.

Some will say this is not true, for I do not want to be sick or poor or unlucky, I just am. I did not want to lose my job or end my relationship but it happened. We are here to say, yes on some level you did believe in this and you can choose to believe differently.

We ask you to focus on appreciation of what is good in your life and not to give your attention on what you lack, and we promise you, what you appreciate will multiply and what you once lacked will no longer be part of your experience.

Attraction Reaction

Attracting what is wanted into this life is so much easier than most believe. We have spent so much of our lives learning that it is hard to get what is wanted, that we believe it is. We want you to know that your belief in difficulties is what is causing your struggle.

Now most find this statement humorous, for how can a belief cause an action? We all believe we want the most and best for ourselves so why do we not have it? We are here to tell you that you do not have it because you really do not believe you can, or you may think you believe you can but deep inside you do not find yourself worthy of receiving.

With so many deep beliefs of disappointing actions how is one supposed to change the way they believe to receive what is wanted? This, dear ones, is where change comes into the picture and to most, change is not easy.

Pay attention to your thoughts but even more, pay attention to your fears. Fears are the disbeliefs that cause you to hold back on receiving. If you are afraid you will not have enough money to pay your bills and you worry how you will get this money... well, it is the worry that is making it difficult for you to be open to the answer that will lead you to creating the money you desire.

We are constantly guiding you to a happier life, if you are worried, scared, angry, jealous, bitter or just feeling sorry for yourself, then you are not in the position to make good on what is wanted. You will not hear the guidance that will change what is not wanted and to receive what is your birthright to be at peace and to be happy with life.

We ask you to start by being at peace with where you are, even if you are not happy with your current situation, for it can get worse and will become more difficult if you do not change for the better. When you are at peace, you allow the ideas that will lead you to your desires. From there you will find that not only do you create a better life but that the life you have is easier for you have no reason to be stressed with worry.

We love you dear ones and know that you get this, for you have been asking and wanting for so long that you are ready for change for the better. Stop believing in difficulties, and be open to receive the guidance that leads you to the desires that you have come here to receive, and to begin to enjoy your life once again.

Chapter Ten

'Manifesting'

A priority based off of correcting 'lack of money' will never amount to making money.

Why Do Some People Seem To Have It All?

You watch your friends, neighbors or even acquaintances and wonder why they are able to have it all, yet you are struggling with the material things you so desire. We say you are not looking at the whole picture, for they have exactly what they have lined up to receive. We ask why have you not done the same? Why have you not aligned yourself with all your material and emotional desires?

You may be asking what is alignment and how do I get there? Alignment is the total understanding and belief that you have what you desire. Easy, right? Well it actually is, other than we have been trained most of our lives not to believe we can do or have anything we so desire, and since that is your aligned belief, well... then that is what you create in your life.

Do you remember when you had created a life experience that you knew you would not give up on until it was achieved? Be it as simple as saving up to buy something, meeting someone, winning something or succeeding at a position or a competition that you desired? You were aligned, you believed no matter what, that would try until you succeeded. If it did not work out as planned, you did not quit for you knew you would do this, and you did. This is what alignment is, and we all have this ability to achieve. This is what we agreed upon and this is our birth right.

Ask And Walk Away

Dear ones, we hear your requests and desires and we say, why ask again (and again) for in doing so you show you do not believe in the outcome.

Once you choose to create or change what is no longer wanted, we ask that you put in your request knowing it is taken care of, and then walk away for you know it is on its way.

When you find yourself praying or asking the universe for the same things again and again, we know you are not ready to receive. And in doing so, you actually push away that which is desired, for your pain of not receiving is equivalent to the belief that it is not coming. For who is sad about asking for something other than those who know it is lacking? AND your belief in lack creates more lack.

We say, believe it is on its way and walk away for there is no need to want something that is coming to you.

We Can Create Healing

Healing is a given gift and our birthright, you know. So, if we can heal ourselves of all these horrible diseases, why are so many plagued by them? This is simple; they do not believe they have any control around it. If they do not believe, it is not possible to create, hence the mind connection.

The body heals with the help of the mind. The mind heals with the help of eternal energy. When the mind believes in the healing, it creates an internal energy that is like our white blood cells. No one questions why white blood cells have the ability to heal but energy – how is that possible? It is possible because everything is made up of energy, including the human body. It is bad energy that can cause a flaw in our health and it is good, positive energy that can repair it.

What We Believe – We Conceive!

Manifestation is all based on belief. What we believe, we conceive. This is the bottom line. Now, getting to the point of believing in something we do not trust in is the difficult part of this all. That is why it takes some many years to trust enough to change their fears.

For many, they truly did not believe they deserve it. That explains most people's fear based beliefs. They want the money, they want the relationship, they want the career or the power but they do not believe they deserve it, and it then will never come. There are many types of blocks, all fear based, you know. All more powerful than the things that are wanted.

Are You Ready To Manifest?

When you are ready for change, you have taken your steps to learn the process (usually by trial and error) and once you have seen the evidence, and you are ready no matter what to succeed, then and only then can the manifestation occur.

Now sometimes you want a change immediately after realizing that you do not like something in your life. You are so sure this is not right for you, your mind set to change is absolute. Then manifestation is easy, there is no doubt, there is only one decision, and it has to manifest.

Manifesting For Dummies

What you believe, you create as your reality. You may think you want money but unless you believe you have money, you will not manifest it. As long as you notice the lack of money and how you never have enough – well then take a look at what you are creating.

You all have the birthright to live well, content and happy lives. We sometimes choose not to accept this and that is okay for we all have freedom of choice and can choose what to believe. The best part is that we also have the freedom of choice to change what we want to believe.

Manifestation 101

We all have stories of manifestation if we think about it. We all believe we are good at something and we create that something to happen – this is manifestation!

So now we want to change something, like a long time belief in lack. If we were able to change our thoughts and trust beyond doubt that there is no lack, then lack would not be able to survive in our mind or in our life. It is that easy.

What makes it hard is that we have thoughts of lack for so long that they have this purpose in our life. So when we decide to change this lack thought and the first lack possibility shows up, we begin to doubt our decision to change, we fall back into our comfort zone of belief of lack, and then the manifestation is no longer possible because we are now creating lack again.

My Favorite Thing To Work Toward – Manifesting

Manifestation is what we all have the ability to do, and most do not know it. It is a 'miracle' to some, yet a 'given' to others. It is easy or impossible depending on how you look at it.

Broken down, manifestation is the creation of thought that is believed. It is that easy. We all have the right to manifest, and many have done so with or without knowing they have. Most like to think it is 'luck' but there is no such thing as good luck or bad, there just is, or the lack of what is.

What we mean by this is that we all manifest but we do not all allow the manifestation into our lives. We have been trained at a young age to believe good things are hard to come by. As long as we continue to believe this, well, we manifest our beliefs so… good things then are hard to come by. Now, if we believe we are lucky or good things happen to us to a point that we do not allow any doubt, then these beliefs will also manifest.

Chapter Eleven

'Relationships'

When you are ready to follow your desires more than you want to please other's opinions; well then you no longer have anything to lose, and life becomes not only easier but more desirable.

Is He/She The One For Me?

You worry about your relationship, or even your lack of relationships and we say that is unnecessary for you are always with the one you should be with. Even if you are alone, this is where you should be. You think you want a loving, caring relationship, but if you really were lined up to be in one, you would be.

This is hard for some to understand because why wouldn't you want to be happy with your soul mate? Dear ones, we want you to know that every relationship that comes into your life is for your benefit, even if it does not last as long as you want it to. The lack of relationship is beneficial also, for it gives you time to know what you truly want.

The reason we are attracted to each other is because the one you line up with, will help you with the life experiences you are working through at the time. That is why we learn from past relationships not to want the same things in the next one. And in the cases where we do not learn, and attract the same unwanted situations, well, then the issues become greater, and usually more painful until we do understand this is not what we want.

Accept what you want from another you share your life with and do not accept that which does not please you for even in the loss of an unwanted relationship is the opportunity for the wanted love to come into your life.

Do not fear that you will never meet the right one, for this blocks you from finding them. We are all unique and we all have the right partner waiting to meet us, we just have to be open and available to do so.

Look At Your Friends

People come in and out of our lives, some are friends, some are acquaintances, some are even strangers. But none of them were by coincidence, not even that person you seen crossing the street. They have all made it to your attention for a reason. This is difficult for some to understand, though it is true.

We attract people who will help us in life, be it a loved one or even an abuser. You think that person who hurt you was none of your doing, but no one can come into your life without your permission.

This being said, what kind of people are you attracting? Do your friends support you, or do they hurt you? Take a close look at how you are treated, and understand that it is you who is attracting this type of behavior.

Once your take responsibility for the people who surround you, knowing you have control over who you let into your life and how you allow yourself to be treated, then you can choose to learn from their kindness or work through the pain that is shared.

My Heart Hurts

Dear ones, we hear your cries and know your pain, but we say it is your choice to hurt, you know. You have given all your power to another, and when the other does not do what you feel they should, then you react in pain.

At times 'Love' is so misused that it should be renamed 'Pain'. We all want to be in love, but the happiness tends to lead into sadness and then we label that Love.

Love is simply you feeling happy with yourself because you use someone else's reaction to you as a reminder of who you really are. In other words, when you first meet someone you like, they make you feel this inner joy. You feel stronger, happier, more confident in yourself. You think if this person likes me, well I must be likable.

Now the truth is that you are likable but not to yourself. You are using this person's opinion of you to like yourself. Then if this person now steps out of line and doesn't do what you want of him/her, then you start to doubt your lovability.

We say, do not use another to like yourself. Do not use another's opinion to see you as you really are. And never, never, never use another to give you what you deserve in life, and then you will never feel your heart hurting for love again.

Why Do We Feel We Need To Be In a Relationship?

We all long for partners, friendship, love, commitment and companionship. We want someone we can talk to and can relate to our lives. This is natural, for we came here to co-exist with others. The problem is that many times our co-existence comes to an end, and we do not accept this ending as a new beginning (as it always is) but as a loss. We then relate the loss and the feelings of emptiness as again. This process will direct ourselves to separate from who we really are and to become whatever it takes to fill the void.

So what makes this need to be in a relationship so strong? Fear – yes, fear. We are afraid of having to move forward alone. We are afraid of learning how to exist on our own after we had spent so much time learning how to exist with another person. We want the comfort of having someone there to help and to listen.

The truth is that every relationship we have is to bring us closer to our life goal. We all came here with a goal or a mission and we attract others to help us in this pursuit. Have we lost you? You thought we were going to talk about the perfect boyfriend or girlfriend and instead we work our way up to your life's goal. Though it is true, if it were not for the experience that brings you toward your mission, you would prefer to be alone.

To Be In A Relationship Or Not

Relationships or the lack of a relationship at times are the same thing. It is all about the bond. There are so many who are in a relationship and there is no bond. They are together in order not to be alone or because they believe they are not good enough to start over and some times, just because they care for the person and do not want to hurt him/her.

Relationships are complicated. There is so much desire to be in a loving relationship that many times we settle just because we want so much to have someone. This does not serve you, for with time your heart will long for the reason you wanted to be in a relationship in the first place.

We ask you to be okay with yourself, to get to know what it is you want in life, to know what it is you are lacking, so you may know what you truly want in your relationship.

Why Do Relationships Hurt?

Many people have hurt pasts that they are trying to correct in future relationships. This actually is not a bad thing because with each lost relationship, more is learned and less of the past history is the current issue. In other words, you are creating new hurts (though similar to the past and original hurt) that are more relevant, and with this action, you are also creating the need to correct it.

This is why you see people who seem to have the same issues in each relationship you have. Yes, they usually get a little better each time but the 'hurt' from the issues tend to feel the same. This is because the pain you feel is never due to the person you are with, it always has to do with your perception of them. No one can ever cause you pain unless you are willing to accept being hurt.

What Are You Looking For In A Relationship?

What is it that you want out of your relationship? If your answer involves any form of being taken care of, then we need to talk. When you look for others to fill a void or a need, you will forever be dependent on them to make you happy, and this is not possible. Someone else can not make you happy, or take care of you, or fix that which really is not broken.

If you are looking for others to help you, it is for one reason only, you have not figured out how to be the person you came here to be. This is okay, for we all get lost on our way, but we never quit trying to find our way. In other words, even if you are not living the life you want, with the people you think you want, being with them will eventually move you toward the direction that brings you joy.

Chapter Twelve

'Thought'

Thoughts create your life –

Think accordingly.

Where Are You Right Now?

Are you happy? Are you wanting for more? We ask this because your state of mind is a result of what you are believing. So many do not understand this, so we will explain.

We are what we think, but it is even more than that, for sometimes we think things we really do not believe. So we are what we think and truly believe. We are given the choice to make our lives what we desire. This was agreed upon before we came to this planet, you know. The problem with most is that they do not even realize that they are desiring to not achieve what they think they want.

We want the perfect relationship, we want lots of money, we want great health and a desirable body... so we think. If your relationship, finances and physical appearance are not what you thought they should be, then think again (literally) for your inner beliefs did create the state you are in, and they can create a change.

Listen to those inner voices when you see others who have what you want, for this is what your beliefs are saying to you. Do you think that loving couples are fools, or that rich people are evil, or that a perfect body must be a result of cosmetic surgery? Change those beliefs! See those (lucky) ones and be truly happy for them, for you KNOW you also will have this.

The truth is, what we really believe, we have no other choice but to create. For what we focus on with belief, is what we will see evidence of. What we see evidence of, is what is drawn toward us. What we are drawn toward, is what we accept as the truth. Which means, what we believe, we will achieve.

Try it, maybe with something small. Be happy that it is coming to you. When you think of it, be excited that you will have it. When you notice the lack of it, let it go for you KNOW this is just temporary. Be sure in your heart that it will come to you in the perfect moment, and that there is no other outcome. Be happy and excited with its future arrival. Trust, as you know it is on its way. Let no other thoughts change your mind, for you are definite in your knowing it is for you. Then just sit back and allow it to come, and we promise it is on its way.

What Do You Choose To Think?

We see what we want to see, because when we believe in something, we only pay attention to what supports it. This, my dear is both beneficial and detrimental. You see, some call it being blind to the truth but we call it creating what is wanted. This is why we ask of you to focus on the good in life, for then that is what will be found.

If you believe in bad, then you will see evidence of bad things everywhere you go. So why do it? Why think bad things happen to you? Why trust in the worse situations until they come true?

It is not easy to change what you are used to, we know. So start small – you have it in you. You know you do, there is a part of you that knows your power, and if you choose to not believe it, or if you have been ignoring it, it can not surface.

What do you want to be true for you? Think about it, feel how good it would feel to have it, pretend you have it, yes we said pretend.   If you continue this, with the good feelings it brings – it has to surface in your life. It is that easy.

Change how you think for the better and a better life will be yours.

Thought Is Everything

Thought is a very powerful thing, much more powerful than people give it credit for. In fact, most think that thoughts are just that, a brief description of an action that passes through their mind. But indeed thought is everything. It is what shapes your life, your beliefs, your direction, your ability to achieve or to destroy what is wanted in life.

Thought is energy and energy is everywhere, so by shifting the energy into the direction of what is wanted or needed, well then it shapes what you desire. So this being said... anything is possible. We lost many with that statement, for most are so limited in their beliefs. This limitation becomes reality because there is energy behind the thought. So by putting this same energy behind a thought of accomplishment or creation, then that is what becomes created.

How Do You Value Success?

Success is all in the mind. One person's success can be another person's failure. The reason success is so important to some, is because they base this state of being as value of themselves. It is comical when broken down and thought through, you know. You work to achieve something in order to believe in your value, but if you valued what you have achieved, no matter how small, then there would be no need to prove anything.

If you start to focus on what is, instead of what is not, then there is only success. It all goes back to what you think about.

Chapter Thirteen

'Why?'

Some feel meditation is the connection to your Higher Energy; we say meditation is the resistance of separation from your Higher Energy.

Why Don't The Puzzle Pieces Fit?

Dear One, your confusion is strong, your focus is weak and your direction has changed. You feel like you are alone in the middle of a thousand people, and you do not know how to be seen. As we say, why be seen? Why not do the looking? Why change what is, when it is there to guide you?

You think that life is the way it is supposed to be but life is what you make of it. Why make it difficult? Why try to help others at the cost of yourself? Pay close attention to how you feel, for if you are hurting, then you are moving in the wrong direction.

Do not force the pieces of the puzzle, for you will end up with an unfinished project. We say put that piece down, for when the time is right, you will know exactly where it belongs.

Life is simple, we then complicate it. Life is happy, we lose trust and make times sad. Life is flowing, and we forget to exhale. Stop that which does not serve you, put your pieces in a row and choose the one which calls you, and you will see, you know exactly where it fits.

What Is The Meaning Of Life?

Do you remember the story of Adam and Eve and the Garden of Eden? They were forbidden to eat from the Tree of Knowledge, but they did. And what happened to them? They were banished from the garden to experience good and evil.

Stories change as they are translated, you know. This story speaks of a decision which changed all of mankind, but was it really that bad? Is experiencing good and evil so much worse than living without experiencing life? These are questions that explain the meaning of life, you know.

When life is difficult, we want someone or something to make it better. What we do not understand is that we all have the power within to make life better. Also, what we really want in life is to be validated, so by having others fix our problems... well, it really can not be done, for the reason we have 'problems' is because we have this desire to move forward in life. The only way we can move forward is to experience the creation of a new, more desirable living. This being said - we want to have problems in life because this is the only way we can find a way of becoming who and what we want.

Why Am I Overweight?

Overweight is different for everyone, but the same to everyone is the need for protection. Protection sounds so serious, we know but it is a very simple concept. There is something that scares you, and instead of facing the fear, you eat the fear away. This is why you call weight gaining food 'comfort foods'. Truly, many can eat the comfort foods and not gain weight. This is because they are not using this food as a crutch. They do not abuse the food and eat it out of content.

So, how do you catch this fear before it is eaten away? Usually when the mindset that losing weight is the most important mission to accomplish. Then you will notice the urge to overeat is there before you eat away the feelings. Now the fear is relevant and emotions surface. This is when you either learn to love yourself (for the fears are usually based off of lack of love and disapproving the self), or you return to your old eating habits.

What Is Meditation And Why Meditate?

Meditation is the calming of the scattered thoughts that get in the way of hearing your inner guidance. Meditation is the relaxing of the body by deep, slow breathing and the concentration of what is. Meditation is the ability to relax to the point of total acceptance of allowing that which flows through you, to be heard.

Some feel meditation is your connection to your Higher Energy; we say meditation is the resistance of separation from your Higher Energy.

Dress comfortably, sit up and relax in a quiet area, close your eyes, take a slow, deep breath through your nose, hold it for just a second and release it slowly through your mouth. **Listen to your breathing. Concentrate on your breaths.** Do this with the intention of surrendering and releasing that which does not serve you. Do this for 15 minutes a day and you will heighten your connection to yourself, as well as to your Higher Energy.

Do You Know Why People Are Selfish?

Do you know why people are selfish? Sometimes life is harder for some than others. They do not know how to deal with feelings that arise, so they fill it with 'stuff'. When they use up their stuff, they are forced to feel what is in that void. This is hard for them, so they hold on to all that they have, trying to fill the void, and trying to stay away from those feelings, you know.

Body, Mind Connection

The body can heal itself of any situation it can get itself into. It can heal cuts, scrapes, broken bones which are things that are easily accepted, we know. But it can also heal itself of diseases, even those that modern medicine can not. This is much harder for some to accept.

The body, mind combination has no limits. It can create beyond belief. In other words, this body, mind ability is what some call miracles. We love that word - miracles, meaning something some can not believe is possible, but has happened so it must be categorized by 'God Himself' going out of His way to make this exception, and create some solution that would have been impossible by 'man himself'. This is easier to believe than we all have the ability to change what is not wanted.

Epilogue

Following your heart is a natural process. Some call it instinct, intuition, inner voice, gut feeling, etc., I call it my inner guidance. We were all born with strong guidance, but as we grew, we were taught the proper way to act and how to function as society believes to be correct.

The problem with this is that we are not all the same, we do not all have the same life experience nor goals. So when you take in consideration what others will think of you, then you begin to forget who you really are.

It is all about choices, if you choose to be happy, life will be more fun. If you choose to worry, life will mimic your thoughts and you will attract more worrisome situations.

Once you figure out that you really do create your own life, then living becomes easier. For you can always choose to redirect your thoughts and beliefs to find your way home again.

Notes